The Retirement Marvel

The Retirement Marvel

The All-in-One Retirement Solution
You've Never Heard Of

Michael Blaker

Expert Press

The Retirement Marvel: The All-In-One Retirement Solution
You've Never Heard Of

ISBN-13: 978-1-946203-24-3

—Disclaimer—

Expert
Press
www.ExpertPress.net

Contents

Of all the words of mice and men, the saddest are,
"It might have been."

~ *Kurt Vonnegut*

1

Looking Back on My Past

IT IS SAID that hindsight is 20/20. I can now tell you with absolute certainty, that statement is true. Everything is so very clear to me now as I look back on my life. I only wish I would have had the vision to see this while I was still alive.

Let me introduce myself. I'm Jonathan Bales. I lived a good life and provided well for my family. I worked hard and put away what I could for retirement. I thought I had everything in place and that my wife and family would be taken care of when I died. One night, I went to sleep and never woke up.

I watched my family grieve, observed my own funeral, and listened intently as the attorney read my will to my family. That's when I realized how much I didn't know.

The dominoes have all fallen and I now understand why things played out in the way they have. Some things have made me happy and some things blindsided me and left me in shock. I never expected some things to work out the way they did. That is the reason behind this book. I want to give you the benefit of my hindsight so that you can avoid being blindsided.

Like many, I saved money a little at a time and added bigger chunks when I was able. In the end, I had a comfortable retirement and some nest eggs tucked away here and there when my journey ended. I never spent those nest eggs because I wanted to be prepared for the unexpected events of life and because I wanted my children to have some financial security left to them when I was gone. If you feel the same way about your nest eggs, then I commend you. You have a responsibility to ensure that the next generation has a good life. However, good intentions are useless without a good plan. That was my mistake.

You see, it is difficult to know what you don't know. It is easy to assume you have all the bases covered based on the knowledge you possess. But what if the picture is much, much bigger than your knowledge base? What if what you have been told all your life isn't the entire picture? What if there are things that you simply do not know or understand? That, my friend, was the fatal flaw in my plans. I didn't know what I didn't know.

There are so many things that can derail a plan. All the good intentions in the world are subject to the details—especially when it comes to leaving an inheritance for your loved ones. The devil *is* in the details.

It is in the details that you discover what I now refer to as the five menaces. These financial foes are the *uninvited, unexpected, unintended, unpredictable,* and *unprepared* aspects of your life and your financial plan.

These five menaces wreaked havoc on my estate and caused much pain and loss for my family. That pain was both emotional and financial. I wouldn't wish that on anyone and it's the core motivation I had in writing this book. I hope you will learn from my mistakes.

My Humble Beginnings

Do you remember your very first job? How much did you make per hour? On my first job in 1950, I picked green beans, corn, and tomatoes for a farmer. This was in Central Illinois when the summer days were a blistering 90-plus degrees with 90 percent humidity. Those were not fun days, but looking back I now know that they were good days. I worked hard and made a good wage at the time: $1.75 per hour.

Can you remember how long it took you to save your first $1,000? $5,000? $10,000? $100,000 or more? Saving money is not easy, but it does pay off in the end.

The ideas in this book are designed to respect what you went through to get where you are today. Whether it's money you saved or money you inherited, that money usually came from blood, sweat, and tears. I want to affirm you for preparing yourself well. I also want to challenge you to do all that you can to preserve what has taken your lifetime to accumulate.

Planning for retirement and leaving a financial legacy to your heirs is a big decision. Before you make any decision like this about your finances, I recommend you ask yourself this question:

"Can this decision hurt me or my family financially?"

I want you to be able to look yourself in the mirror and say with absolute conviction and no regrets,

> *"I have done all I could possibly do to be a good steward of what God has given me. I have a good income that not only I, but my wife also, can count on for a lifetime. Our money is safe, protected from lawsuits, risk, and to the best of my ability . . . uninvited heirs. My kids will not be burdened with unexpected increases in taxes as I have provisions to leave them tax-free, probate-free cash as part of their inheritance. And they'll never have to worry about being unprepared for an unintended illness or accident that would put undue stress on them since I have provided for long-term care protection should we need it."*

Let me encourage you to take action before it's too late and be responsible to change what you can now. If something has a negative effect on your estate, don't let the mirror tell you it was your fault.

This book will not only help you assess where your estate stands now, but also help you determine what adjustments you can make to protect your assets, ensure your income, and provide for your heirs. You and your rightful heirs deserve that peace of mind. The last thing you want your family to find out is that there is another heir to your estate that they didn't know about: an heir who will take away a large portion of the money you intended to go to your family.

Let me tell you about the *uninvited* guest who showed up at the reading of my will.

"When the flower blooms, the bees come uninvited."

~ Ramakrishna

2

The Uninvited Guest

A FEW DAYS after my funeral, my family was gathered to hear my last wishes and how my estate was to be divided. It was a private meeting with our family attorney that was very somber. Can you imagine the shock and I anger I felt when an uninvited "heir" showed up during the reading of my will?

Not long after this meeting began, the door swung open and in he walked. Not only did he have the audacity to show up to this private, family gathering, but he elbowed his way to the front of the room and demanded the lion's share of my estate!

My wife and children objected and demanded he leave. It was apparent he had no intention of going anywhere. Instead, he slammed down some papers on the attorney's desk, pointed to a specific section, and glared at all of us before he greedily smiled and assumed his position as the primary heir of my estate.

He wanted his portion of my estate and he got it.

My children were forced to split up what remained. I was shocked! I had no idea that this uninvited guest actually had claim to a large part of my nest egg and that the government and the law would back him 100 percent. Looking back, I can now see what I could have done to not only keep this uninvited intruder from being an heir, but also how to guarantee that my family received every penny I intended for them to have.

In the pages that follow I'll share with you what I've learned from my new perspective. I trust it will be helpful as you plan your financial future.

Preventing Health and Money Problems

I know how confusing estate planning can seem. What I now realize is that it's really very simple. It's just like taking care of your physical health.

Think about it. Good physical health requires:

- Seeking preventive care
- Eating a balanced diet
- Avoiding things we know can hurt us
- Promoting that which keeps us safe
- Keeping close to God—the closer, the better

In the same way, good financial health can include:

- Seeking professional advice
- Insuring your money
- Insuring your income
- Insuring your spouse's income
- Protecting your estate from long-term care expense
- Protecting your heirs' inheritance from going to someone else
- Avoiding what can deplete your assets or your income

You probably get an annual physical—at least I hope you do. You also need an annual financial check-up. In both cases, you want to be proactive about your care.

If during your annual physical checkup your doctor told you he detected a small bit of skin cancer, when would you want to start treatment? Would you start immediately, or would you let it grow for a few months before taking action?

I know, that's a silly question. But if the answer is so obvious, why don't we make the same decision with our financial health?

During a physical exam, lab results can detect problem areas in our chemistry, while x-rays and ultrasounds can give our doctors essential information they need to make a proper diagnosis. A similar process happens when you meet with a qualified financial advisor who is looking out for the financial health of your family.

Your life is not just about you. It's about your spouse if you have one; it's about your kids, your grandkids, and your great-grandkids. Preventive medicine can change lives. So can preventive financial planning. You need to have an annual check-up both physically and financially.

This is another area where I didn't do what was best for my family.

When I was planning for my retirement, I listened to the advice of the majority. It seemed like everyone was on the same road heading in the same direction. I talked with a few different advisors, watched the market, read some books, and thought I had everything taken care of. I would give my financial health a solid B. Good enough for a normal guy like me (I never was an over-achiever).

Looking back, I now see that my grade was actually a C-. Yes, I did some things right, but there were a few places where I could have made some small changes that would have produced a much better outcome. I now understand what I could have done differently and how those few small changes would have given me a B+, or perhaps even an A. That would have placed my family in a much better position going forward. I'll share a few of those with you in the coming pages.

So as you consider your future, be sure you are focusing on preventing problems with your health *and* your money. These are far too important to take them for granted. And if you simply listen to the majority, or what "they" tell you, you're setting yourself up to experience an unintended loss.

"Too often, we miss out on opportunities in this life because we were too busy waiting for them to fall into our lap that we missed them tapping on our shoulder."

~ *Daniel Willey*

3

The Unintended Loss

I'VE LEARNED THAT there are literally trillions of dollars in banks across the country lying dormant in a product we are all familiar with. It's called a certificate of deposit (CD). These CDs are like a parking lot for your money. You give your money to the bank for a very small amount of interest, and they promise to give it back to you at some later date. We like them because of their safety. But have you ever thought of the unintended loss that goes with every CD?

The question is why would someone put money in a CD when the interest paid on these accounts is extremely low and there's no tax advantage or other benefit to the account holder?

When your money is in a CD it doesn't grow much. It isn't working for you. It's like floating on an inner tube in a water park on one of these lazy rivers. Money that you invest is supposed to work for you to earn you more money. So why do so many people choose these "lazy money" places to park their money?

First, let's understand what we mean by "lazy money." In short, "lazy money" is any type of savings account or investment vehicle where your money isn't working for you. It doesn't do much; it just sits there. It sits around all day and does nothing. It's lazy! Sure, it's always there, inside the house where it is safe and sound, even ready if you need it, but for the most part, it does nothing.

The ironic part about lazy money is that it's actually quite busy and working very hard. The problem is that it's working hard for someone else, typically the bank or the financial institution that holds your money.

Did you know that banks, by federal regulation, can loan out up to 10 times the amount of your deposit? Can you imagine your bank loaning out your money to earn 18 percent interest or more on credit card loans, but only paying you less than one percent? That's what they are doing with your "lazy money."

So if that's the case, why on earth do so many people choose these lazy money places to park their funds when logic tells us it doesn't make any sense?

Well, the answer is threefold.

First is safety. People want to know their money is safe and most people perceive banks as a safe place to hold their money, mainly because of FDIC insurance.

The second reason is accessibility. Most people want the peace of mind knowing if they need to make a withdrawal in case of an emergency, or they simply need additional cash, all they need to do is drive down to the bank. The ironic part about that is most of the money sitting in CDs and savings accounts is never actually withdrawn until a life-changing event occurs.

Lastly, people put money in lazy money places because it's convenient. Think about it: there's a bank on nearly every corner in every town in America. It doesn't get more convenient than that.

There's also one more important reason why there's so much lazy money sitting in banks today. People simply don't know any other options—I sure didn't. The choice seems to be either the bank or the stock market. And for many people the latter is not a consideration at all.

When you park your money in a CD or some other type of lazy money location, the unintended loss you have is that your money works really hard for someone else, but not for you. They gain and you lose. That's the bad news. The good news is there's a better way. I call it the money snowball.

The Money Snowball

If you've ever had the fun of making a snowman this analogy will make a lot of sense. To make a snowman, you begin with a small snow ball. As you roll that snowball, the motion adds more snow and soon you have a much larger ball. This becomes the base of your snowman. Repeat this process a couple more times and you have a beautiful snow man.

But if you simply make a snowball, place it in the snow and leave it there, it will stay a snowball. It is the movement or motion of the snowball that adds snow and creates the snowman.

The same is true with your money. If you place your money in a bank and just leave it there where these is no motion, then you'll just keep your money. But if you put your money in motion, your "money snowball" will add more money to it and you'll end up with a much larger sum of money that is still safe.

A Safe Harbor

What if there were an alternative parking place for money whereby the saver—YOU—could experience the same (if not better) protection/ insurance than the FDIC provides, have greater access to your savings with an unconditional money back guarantee and enjoy additional benefits such as higher interest, extra money (yes, extra money—as much as two and half times the amount of your deposit) to be used for extended care such as assisted living expenses and nursing home costs?

And what if that same money could also provide a tax-free inheritance to your heirs (not some uninvited guest) in the event of your death (often as much as double your initial deposit)?

This "money snowball" is possible because your money is put into motion so that it continues to grow while being protected from the unexpected risks that hurt so many.

I'm here to tell you that there IS a place like this where you can put your money at work for you, not the bank. A place where your money is safe, accessible, and where it grows year after year and earns more and more money for you and your heirs on a tax-free basis.

Why have you not heard about this option before? Because the uninvited guest who showed up at the reading of my will wants to come to the reading of your will also. He doesn't want you to know about this.

In fact, if you have not planned properly, he's already your number one heir. And believe me, he's greedy and aggressive and he will get every penny he asks for unless you take action to protect your family and your estate.

The bottom line is that banks are great for our transactional needs, such as cash, checks, paying bills, etc. But they were never designed to provide people with more growth or protection from an unpredictable future.

If you store your money in a bank, the unintended loss you'll realize is that your money is not growing because, although it is in a very safe place, it is not gaining much interest (you still have a snowball). You won't be building your investments to protect yourself from the unexpected events that may occur in the future, and you will be unprepared to provide lifetime income for your spouse should they outlive you.

Please hear me . . . I am not anti-bank. In fact, I had some money in our local bank. I've just come to realize that there are better places for retirement nest eggs than the local bank.

If you want your Money Snowball to become a snowman, then your money needs to be put into motion where YOU are gaining the benefits. There is a way to do this that is simple, easy to understand, and very safe. Millions of people have used these accounts for many years and not one of them has ever ended up wishing they had done something else. Having the peace of mind that comes with a safe, secure plan for your family is priceless. And the good news is that it is well within your reach.

For you to avoid the unintended loss of your money not working for you, you need to make sure that your money is working <u>for</u> you and is growing safely to provide for you and your family for generations to come.

But creating a large Money Snowman is not the only objective. You need to protect your family from someone running off with a large portion of your estate. That's why you need to make the commitment now so that you will not be unprepared for this uninvited guest because as you now know, his appearance at the reading of your will is no longer unexpected.

"*Government's view of the economy could be summed up in a few short phrases: If it moves, tax it. If it keeps moving, regulate it. And if it stops moving, subsidize it.*"

~ *Ronald Reagan*

4

The Unexpected Cost

LET ME ASK YOU something. At the end of your life, what do you want to leave to your heirs? Perhaps a better question would be: How much of what you leave them do you want them to share with the IRS?

I suspect your answer to the second question is nothing. So if it were possible for you to disinherit the IRS—and do so morally, legally, and ethically—would you let me show you how?

If you answered yes, keep reading.

Would you like to guess who the "uninvited guest" was at the reading of my will? Yep, the IRS. Here's why he showed up.

The Ps and Qs of Retirement Income

In the early 1970s the U.S. government looked down the road and saw that they would need a lot of money for a very long time. Now the government only has one source of income: taxes. And raising taxes is not a popular thing to do. So, being sly, the government created as part of the IRS tax code, section 401(k), which basically allowed individuals to invest (or contribute) into their retirement account on a tax-deferred basis.

The upside is that the contributions you made were deductible on your taxes when you made them, thus reducing your taxable income. That's good.

The downside (which they didn't explain very well on purpose) is that the IRS <u>deferred</u> the taxes on all of the gains you would have until you were ready to access your money when you retire. Thus, you will pay taxes on the gains you have realized over the years.

The IRS knew there would be much more money for them if they allowed you to <u>defer</u> the tax on your money than if they taxed you when you put the money in your account (A few years later the Roth IRA was created and it does allow you to pay taxes now and not later, but most people are faced with the unexpected cost of <u>deferred</u> taxes that come with a traditional IRA).

What this means is that the IRS is your number one heir and will deplete much of your retirement savings unless you do something about it.

Listening to Grandpa (The "P" of Retirement Income)

As a boy, I remember visiting my grandparents. They weren't rich, yet they never seemed to worry about money. I asked Grandpa about this one day and he told me that he had a pension. I asked him what that was. He said it was a retirement paycheck that he would receive every month for the rest of his life.

No wonder he never worried about money. He had guaranteed income for life. That sounded like great idea at the time. I only wish now that I would have spent more time listening to grandpa and remembered his advice, then followed in his footsteps.

Qualified Plans (the "Q" of Retirement Income)

With the onset of the IRA (Individual Retirement Account) the retirement income for most Americans has shifted away from monthly pension checks from employers and has moved to income they draw from their own retirement accounts, such as 401(k) accounts, IRAs, and other such "qualified" plans.

They are called "qualified" plans because they qualify for tax deductions upfront, AND they qualify the IRS to become your number one heir when you die.

Since their inception, it is estimated that trillions of dollars have been invested in these "qualified accounts" that began back in the mid-1970s. It's about all we've heard of in our lifetime. Looking back on my life, it's no wonder I didn't know that there was another place I could put my money so that it would grow safely and provide protection for my family without the IRS getting their unfair share of my estate. "They" didn't want me to know about it because then "they" would not get any of my money.

The reality is that when you are ready to take your money out of your qualified plan, or give it to your heirs, the Tax Man shoves his way to the front and demands his portion first. Believe me, you do not want what happened to me to happen to you.

In the U.S., fully one quarter to one third of the money in these qualified accounts goes *not* to the heirs in a will, but to the IRS at one's death when a beneficiary other than a spouse or a charity receive them.

I can assure you that given a choice, every beneficiary (heir) that I've ever known would much prefer the government not get a dime of what's coming to them, and the heir desires all of what they are to receive to come to them on a tax-free basis.

Additionally, when people retire and begin enjoying the income from their qualified accounts, they sometimes find themselves in a tax situation that they did not see coming.

We're told that we'll most likely be in a *lower* tax bracket when we retire, but that's not always the case.

The money you've put away on a pre-tax basis has enjoyed years of tax-deferred growth and is now yours for the taking, but 100 percent of the income from these qualified accounts is subject to income tax.

Maybe you say this is no big deal, since you aren't working anymore, but let's look at the whole picture. Yes, you are retired. In your retirement, you may enjoy a pension (like my grandpa), some money from Social Security, and a stream of income from your qualified accounts. Many people find themselves in retirement actually having an income equal to or in excess of their income when they worked full time. That can pose an *unexpected* tax problem.

The average person at retirement has paid off their house. They have raised and educated their children, and if they had a business, they've either sold it or closed it down. I mention the house, the children, and the business for good reason, as all three can offer substantial tax breaks.

So if someone is blessed enough to enjoy a well-funded retirement in the absence of these three tax deductions, you can probably guess what their income tax situation might look like. It's higher than they expected.

How then do we enjoy the fruits of our labor without giving the Tax Man his unfair share of our earnings? Let me share with you a few ways I've learned to do this.

Not long ago, a man told me that he wasn't at all worried about taxes or his income. His reasoning? He had substantial losses in the market. He could carry over these losses for the next five years, almost assuring him a tax-free status. (For the record, I do not recommend this as a strategy, and I'm no financial genius.)

Of course if you are over 65 and keep your gross income below $11,900 as an individual and $23,200 as a couple, you probably will pay no income taxes. If this income suits you, then all is well, but if you have an income that is higher than this, you'll want to plan properly so you will not pass your tax problem on to your kids and grandkids as so many people do.

How does this happen?

According to the Life Insurance Marketing and Research Association (LIMRA) Secure Retirement Institute, $117.4 billion went into fixed annuities in 2016, along with approximately $113 billion in variable annuities outside of Roth accounts. All of the earnings—100 percent—in an annuity are tax deferred, but are subject to income tax once withdrawn. According to some estimates, approximately 85 percent of these annuities are never touched by the annuity owner.

Consider the case of Betty.

Betty (age 80) has $200,000 of annuities. She has owned these annuities for over 15 years. She originally invested $100,000 and has watched her money double on a tax deferred basis. (She does not need the income from these accounts to live on). Her concern is the amount of income tax her heirs will pay on the $100,000 of tax deferred gains on the annuities.

Her solution was very simple and beneficial to both her and her heirs. Please read the following letter that Betty wrote to her children. How would you feel if you did the same type of planning for your family? How would they remember you? Many of you have a choice. You can leave a taxable inheritance to your heirs or a tax-free inheritance. The choice is yours.

Dear Kids,

I am writing this letter to let you know of a financial concern in my estate. I currently have approximately $200,000 in my annuities. The concern I am talking about is that 100 percent of the gain in the annuities is subject to income taxes. Currently you would owe the IRS an estimated $30,000 of income tax on my annuities prior to you using these funds.

To solve this tax concern I recently decided to do some arbitrage using life insurance. This life insurance policy will provide you with $340,000 of tax free, probate-free cash. The life insurance policy that I am talking about will increase your after-tax inheritance from $170,000 with annuities to $340,000. An increase of $170,000 or 100 percent.

In addition to the benefits payable to you, I get $130,000 of long term care coverage and $200,000 of terminal illness coverage. I also have access to 90 percent of the cash that builds up in the plan.

So you see kids, this plan is beneficial to you and me. I cannot think of a safer more tax-advantaged way to invest. I've been *told that Malcolm Forbes had $55,000,000 of life insurance in force when he died. Not a bad example to follow I must say.*

Lots of Love, Mom

Another way tax burdens are passed to the next generation is with qualified money. I have had many friends tell me that if they didn't have to take a required minimum distribution (RMD) from their IRA, they would prefer to just let the money sit in their IRA and continue to grow. In these cases, qualified plan withdrawals by people age 70 ½ are usually limited to the required minimum, and after time the bulk of the IRA is still intact at death.

The IRS is very gracious when a spouse leaves IRA funds to the surviving spouse. According to IRS publication 590A a spouse can treat an inherited IRA as their own. However, that same publication also states very clearly that "If you inherit a traditional IRA from anyone other than a deceased spouse, you cannot treat the IRA as your own." In other words, the IRS is going to tax that money.

Did you know that you can use a portion of your IRA to help your heirs with these taxes? It occurs when you use a portion of your IRA money to purchase another product that provides tax-free money to your heirs. This process of using a portion of your assets to invest in another asset is called arbitrage.

Many people are unprepared for the reality that awaits them. They believe that since they have set up a trust, all is well. I've seen that is not always the case.

Far too often that trust has been named the primary beneficiary of a traditional IRA for the purpose of avoiding probate and having the funds equitably divided among the heirs. But without special circumstances in a trust, it is possible that the trust will have to pay income tax at a corporate rate on all the qualified funds as those funds come into the trust. That means less money for your heirs and more money for the IRS.

If avoiding probate is the motive for leaving these funds to the trust, there are other effective ways to accomplish that. For example, add a P.O.D. (payable on death) or T.O.D (transfer on death) stipulation to the trust account. You may use insurance products or other products that allow for named beneficiaries. You also may want to remember the phrase *per stirpes*. This is a Latin phrase that literally means "by roots." In legal and financial terms, it means that money will follow the blood line.

Let me explain. Many of my friends have a spouse, children, and grandchildren. Usually the spouse is named as the primary beneficiary and children as contingent beneficiaries, more often than not in equal shares. Per stirpes applies when one of the beneficiaries dies before the individual whose estate is being divided.

For example, I asked one of my friends the tough question of how things were to be done should one of her children precede her in death. Would she want her surviving children to get an additional share or her grandchildren from the deceased child to get their parent's share? She said she would want her grandchildren from her deceased child to get their share. Then she began to cry. I am not in the habit of making my 80-year-old friends cry. When I asked her what was wrong, she said that had happened to her. Her father passed away before his own father did. Her grandfather lived another 10 years after her dad passed. After her grandpa died, my client watched the entire estate go to her aunts and uncles. Nothing went to her or her siblings. She looked at me and asked, "Why do you think Grandpa disinherited me?" I had no answer except to say that perhaps whoever was doing the estate planning for her grandpa did not understand how important adding per stirpes to a beneficiary arrangement can be. I will never forget the look on this woman's face and I pray it will never be the look on your face.

Another answer to my question of how to help the heirs with the tax problem on traditional IRAs is: "We've taken care of that with a stretch IRA." (A stretch IRA is a specially designed IRA that your financial advisor can explain to you).

It is true that this may initially lessen the burden of income tax on inherited qualified money. Still, 100 percent of the distributions from a traditional IRA are subject to income tax. In my opinion, spreading the taxes out over the beneficiary's lifetime only makes the duration for paying taxes on these funds longer—in this case a lifetime—without necessarily reducing the amount of the taxes. There may be some tax-free options that can be used. A good friend of mine, Tom, has a wonderful story about this:

Tom, an 82 year old widower with four grown children and seven grandchildren, has approximately $350,000 in his IRA account. Tom takes a required minimum distribution from his IRA because he must, not because he needs the income. One of his goals is to leave a financial legacy to his family.

Please read the following letter that he wrote to his children. Again, how would you feel if you did the same type of planning for your family? How do you think Tom feels now?

Dear Kids,

I am writing this letter to let you know of a financial concern in my estate. I currently have approximately $350,000 in my IRA. The concern I am talking about is that 100 percent of these funds are subject to income taxes. Currently you would owe the IRS an estimated $100,000 of income tax on my IRA prior to you using these funds.

To solve this tax concern I recently started a program of arbitrage using life insurance. This life insurance policy will provide you with $500,000 of tax free, probate-free cash. The life insurance policy that I am talking about will increase your after tax inheritance from $250,000 with the IRA to $500,000. That's an increase of $250,000 or 100 percent. *

In addition to the benefits payable to you I get $200,000 of long term care coverage and $250,000 of terminal illness coverage. I also have access to 90 percent of the cash that builds up in the plan.

So you see kids, this plan is beneficial to you and me. I cannot think of a safer more tax-advantaged way to invest. I've been *told that Malcolm Forbes had $55,000,000 of life insurance in force when he died, not a bad example to follow I must say.*

Lots of Love, Dad

In my opinion, if someone can qualify, life insurance purchased with the after-tax withdrawals from an IRA is often the most beneficial solution to this big tax problem. After all, if you were my beneficiary, is there anything I could leave you that would be better than tax-free, probate-free cash? That's one of the great benefits of a properly structured life insurance policy.

According to IRS publication 525 (shown on next page) there is no income tax due on the proceeds of life insurance, unless the policy is turned over to you for a price. (That is, unless you start buying and selling life insurance policies as a business.) In effect, the tax savings of life insurance helps fund the cost of the insurance itself.

Partners for Life

When my wife and I married, we became partners for life. There was nothing that could separates us except death. I thought we were the only ones who had this type of relationship. I now know that's not the case.

If you are investing in a "qualified plan" like an IRA, you also have a partner for life, but it's not with your spouse. Besides the company with which your IRA is invested, who is your other partner? If you guess the IRS, you guessed correctly. Why is this? Because the government allowed you to invest your money on a <u>tax-deferred</u> basis. The catch is that they are due the taxes on the growth of your money when you withdraw it. The IRS knew that they could either tax you on the little that you were putting in (the seed), or on a much larger portion when you took it out (the harvest). They never really told you about that, did they?

But what if you could find a Partner for Life who wouldn't deceive you and who would actually treat you honestly? A partner who would allow you to invest your money, allow it to grow, and take it out tax free? The good news is I know of a partner like this.

You may not believe me (I know I would have been skeptical) but this honest partner is an insurance company.

Consider for a moment what the IRS will do for your family with the taxes paid versus what the insurance company will do for you and your family. Often times my friends have actually been able to use a life insurance policy to double their loved ones' inheritance and get accelerated benefits to pay for such things as home health care, long term care, assisted living, adult day care, and even terminal illness.

Depending on how the policy is set up (you need to work with an advisor who understands your situation and how to properly structure this policy so it will provide and protect your family exactly the way you want it to) a properly structured insurance policy can actually do multiple things at one time. It's like starting with a snowball and rolling it around to make a snowman. These types of policies are how you can create your Money Snowman.

Please don't dismiss this idea too quickly. You may not have all the information you need, and you may have been misled by others. I know that I was. If I knew then what I know now, I would have made a few very different decisions. This would be one of them.

Given a choice between the IRS and a major insurance company as a Partner for Life, my wise friends chose the insurance company. I wish I would have, also.

"Prepare for the unknown by studying how others in the past have coped with the unforeseeable and the unpredictable."

~ *George S. Patton*

5

The Unpredictable Future

LET ME TALK to the responsible husbands for a moment as we take a critical look at how you are providing for your spouse to have income for life after you are gone. Statistics show that women tend to live longer than men, and so many women outlive their spouses. What this means is that most likely, your wife will live longer than you do and it is your responsibility to ensure she has enough income to live the rest of her life without worry.

This subject is very personal to me. Both of my grandmothers were widowed and my mother is also a widow. I take this matter very seriously. Every married couple needs to be asked this question: "What two things in life are absolutely certain?" The most common answers are death and taxes.

If we agree that death and taxes are certainties in life, then we should ask, "What is the economic impact of you or your spouse surviving each other?" When asked this question, 95 percent of people look at each other and say, "We don't know."

Let me share a couple of stories with you.

A few years ago I was visiting with a couple in Sedona, Arizona. They had attended a financial planning seminar and asked if they could meet with the advisor when he had finished the presentation.

They shared with the advisor that the husband was a retired minister and that he got a $4,000 per month pension. He also had qualified for $1,000 monthly from Social Security as did his wife. Between his pension and the two Social Security checks they received a total of $6,000 per month.

When they were asked how the husband took his pension, the retired minister replied that he had taken his full pension. The advisor immediately knew what this meant, as did the husband; only the wife was unsure.

When the wife was asked if she knew the meaning of what her husband of 40 years had just said she said she had no idea.

The advisor then looked at her husband and said, "Please tell her what it means that you have taken your full pension." He gave a look that should have been captured on video. He asked him a second time to please explain to his wife how his pension was designed.

Again, a dirty look and more silence. The advisor then said, "Please, I know this isn't easy, but she deserves to know." With a scowl on his face he said to his wife, "Honey, if you survive me, you don't get any of my pension."

I wish that her expression had been captured also; it was a look of total disbelief. She replied, "What do you mean I don't get any of your pension?" He said, "Remember when I retired 15 years ago? I brought home the paperwork and you signed it." My guess is that he went home with his pension paperwork and said, "Honey, I need you to sign these papers so I can start getting my pension next month." She said to me, "I just can't believe this is true."

The advisor replied, "Ma'am, I am afraid it's even worse. You see, Social Security is not going to continue to send you two checks for $1,000 monthly. You will only get one of the two." You could have knocked her out of her chair with a feather. She said to her husband, "Let me get this straight. If I outlive you, my income will go from $6,000 a month to $1,000 a month? How am I going to live on $1,000 a month? I can't believe I am going to lose $5,000 a month.

What am I going to do?" Her husband responded with a shrug of the shoulders.

This woman was completely unprepared for this news. It was unexpected and she was shocked and frightened about her now very unpredictable future.

The advisor said, "Ma'am, this situation is not at all uncommon, and I have committed a great deal of time and energy to find a solution for it. Would it give you peace of mind to know that in many cases we can fix this problem and restore your widow's income to what you were receiving as a wife?"

He was now her new best friend. She said, "That would be wonderful if you could do that."

Looking at the husband the advisor said, "Would it be alright with you if I show you how I have helped several of my clients fix a similar problem? He looked at him with a straight face and said, "Oh, don't worry about it. I already have a plan." The advisor replied with a bit of surprise in his voice, "You do? That's great. Please tell me your plan." He replied, "If anything happens to me, she can just marry one of the deacons in the church."

As ridiculous as this may sound, he was serious. He refused to take any advice to purchase life insurance with a portion of his passive assets to protect the income of his wife of 40 years. They got up and walked out never to be seen again.

My heart goes out to that poor wife. He husband was not looking out for her and I can only imagine the pain and sorrow she felt from that day forward. It doesn't have to be this way.

How many other spouses have this same sad fate brought on by the misguided and often absurd plans of a perhaps well-meaning spouse who because of pride or any number of other reasons rejects wise counsel?

If you're married, I implore you to let your advisor do an assessment to determine the economic impact of losing a spouse. Please do this now before it's too late to fix any problems.

Then there's the couple in Scottsdale I'd like to tell you about who are on the other side of this equation and did a great job with their estate planning.

Let's call them Sally and Bill. Sally was three years younger than Bill and stood to lose $3,000 of their $5,000 monthly income if she survived him. If Sally were to outlive her husband by 10 years and lose $36,000 per year, that's a whopping $360,000 of lost income. When they learned this from their very wise financial advisor, he asked if he could show them how to insure their at-risk income as they would insure any other valuable asset. They said, "Yes."

Most of people agree that if their home was valued at $360,000 they would insure it for replacement value. Last time I checked, the odds of a home burning down was approximately 1 in 2,500. What are odds of dying some day? 100 percent! And aren't husbands and wives more valuable than a house?

Bill was quick to point out that if Sally survived him she had a $400,000 home that was paid for and $300,000 of investments to fall back on. He made it very clear that if the $300,000 was not adequate to support her lifestyle that she could sell the house and move into a small apartment or move in with their kids. To Bill's surprise, Sally said there was no way she would move in with the kids.

Their advisor said, "Bill, with all due respect, let me say that the difference between you and my clients is the fact that if my clients end up selling their home it's because they want to not because they need to. Besides, there is no guarantee that the $300,000 will be there for her when you are gone." When he asked what this meant the advisor explained that many Americans find themselves in need of long-term care (LTC) or home health care before they die. Since none of us can guarantee that it won't happen to us, there's no reason to be unprepared. The unexpected may indeed come knocking on your door. That's why it's important to do some planning to preserve assets and let someone else—like an insurance company—pay these expenses. He was quick to say that it wouldn't be a problem because his kids would take care of him.

That's a very typical response. Yet the unintended reality is that such a decision puts an enormous burden on our children and grandchildren. It's a burden that is easily avoided with proper planning. For example, let's say my doctor, after my being hospitalized for two weeks, called a family meeting and told us that I was being discharged from the hospital in 48 hours, but I could not go home unattended. He made the choices clear. One of my kids could move in with me and start bathing me, changing my diapers, and feeding me or I could move in with them and they could care for me in the convenience of their home. As much as I love my kids and I am confident they love me, which one of the four do you think is going to be the one to volunteer for such a demanding commitment? Even if one of them were willing, I would not be at all comfortable with such an arrangement, as I am sure they would not either.

I can't begin to tell you the peace of mind you can have knowing that not only is the income that you bring in to your household insured but so is the contingent liability of LTC expense. By handing that responsibility off to a major insurance company who is far better equipped to pay such expenses than you will ever be, you'll sleep like a baby every night of your retirement years.

Since I shared this information with Sally and Bill I am happy to report that they moved forward with the planning necessary to protect each other's income and their estate from LTC expense and unnecessary income tax. Even though neither Sally nor Bill ever had a family member need LTC they decided it was better to be safe than sorry. They were no longer unprepared for an unpredictable future.

Looking back on my life I can see where I did not plan as well as I could have. My wife and my heirs suffered unintended consequences because of the unexpected heirs of my estate (the IRS) and how unprepared I left them for the future. Oh, if only I could make some different decisions. It's too late for me to make any changes, but it's not too late for you. By acting now you can become a champion of protection for your family.

"A champion is afraid of losing.
Everyone else is afraid of winning."

~ *Billie Jean King*

6

The Undisputed Champion

WHEN I WAS growing up, Mohammad Ali was the undisputed champion of the world in boxing. No one could beat him. There are undisputed champions in many fields, including planning for your retirement.

In my later years, I now wish that I would have known about the undisputed champion of retirement and estate planning. The plan I had was a contender, but it wasn't all I needed it to be.

Through the pages of this book I've shared some of my life and told you about some of my friends and the decisions they made. These have been nice stories, but let's get to the point.

Let's assume that you enjoy good health and have discretionary income. If you could design the perfect retirement vehicle, it should include the following features:

1) Tax-free income at retirement
2) Tax-free access to your money (even prior to age 59 ½) for such things as buying or remodeling a home, educating your children, weddings, car purchases, college, or anything else you deem to be reasonable and prudent. It's your money after all. YOU should have access to use it when you want for whatever you want without penalty.
3) Protection in the event you become disabled

By paying taxes now and using after-tax money to fund this plan we get tax-deferred growth, tax-free access to our principal and interest, and protection of the principal in the case of disability. I know this sounds confusing, but when you sit down with a qualified financial advisor, they'll help it all make sense. It's simply too complex to explain through these pages. Believe me when I tell you, this is one conversation you must have.

Now you may be asking, "What product offers all of these benefits?"

It's called **Single Deposit Insurance (SDI)**. Basically, instead of making monthly payments over a number of years, you make a single deposit (hence, the name) and begin enjoying all of these benefits immediately.

Not only can you enjoy great benefits for yourself, consider the tax savings your heirs will enjoy when they receive their inheritance tax free. Most people estimate that if your IRA or other qualified plan had $1,000,000 in it, the taxes your heirs would pay would be approximately $350,000. Remember how my "uninvited guest" elbowed his way to the front of the room to get his portion of the inheritance? In this case, he'd receive the entire $350,000 and your heirs would be left with $650,000 instead of $1,000,000.

But when you have a properly structured Single Deposit Insurance policy protecting you and your money, you can exclude the Tax Man completely and the entire $1,000,000 benefit will go to your heirs completely tax free!

When people are first presented with this option their typical response goes something like this:

"You're kidding, right? You're recommending that I buy permanent life insurance at my age? No way! I am 78 years old, my house is paid for, and my kids are all through with college and on their own. I've paid cash for my cars since before I can remember. I pay off my credit cards in full every month. I have over $400,000 of investments. Why in the heck would I be at all interested in permanent life insurance? Give me one good reason."

This is when a wise, cool-headed advisor calmly says, "Okay, I'll give you several reasons now that I've had the chance to review your financial status and discuss your financial goals.

First, let's talk about your wife. You've been married 58 years. If she survives you, as many women do, she will lose half of your $4,000 monthly pension. She will also lose her $1,500 monthly Social Security check. This is $3,500 monthly or $42,000 yearly of lost income. She will lose this income every year for the rest of her life. If she survives you for 10 years she will lose $420,000. That amount is greater than your current investment portfolio. Ask yourself, and ask your wife, is this an insurable interest? Most everyone agrees that it is.

Secondly, you have over $200,000 of IRAs. My question to you is how much of what you don't spend in your lifetime do you want your family to share with the IRS? Currently, your family will owe approximately $60,000 to the IRS for income taxes due on your IRA. Given a choice, do you think your family would prefer to settle the estate using taxable or tax-free money? My guess is they would choose, and rightfully so, to settle the estate using tax-free money. Here then, is our second reason why life insurance makes sense. You see, life insurance is not subject to income tax in most cases.

You also have approximately $200,000 of non-IRA money in tax-deferred annuities. According to the IRS, 100 percent of the deferred gains are taxable when they are withdrawn from the annuities. The tax is paid by you and your wife if the two of you make the withdrawals. If your heirs make the withdrawals, they pay the income tax. Either way, income tax will be applied on 100 percent of the deferred annuity gains. Your original deposit in the annuity was $100,000. This portion is your cost basis and is income-tax-free. However, there are $100,000 of deferred gains that are subject to income tax. This will create an income tax bill of approximately $30,000. Rather than share the inheritance with the IRS, you could morally, legally, and ethically disinherit them by settling the estate with tax-free, probate-free cash generated by life insurance."

Another thing to consider is the need for long-term care (LTC). In 2013, the John Hancock company did a study and determined that 70 percent of Americans over 65 will need some type of LTC during their lifetime. Most of the plans my wise friends put in place protected their assets from these costs and allowed them to pay for this care using someone else's money (the insurance company's).

These friends have great peace of mind knowing that needed care will be there should they need it, *and* it will be paid for by using someone else's money (the insurance company will pay for this when your SDI policy is structured properly). Again, this is just one of the benefits that life insurance can provide.

You may have outgrown the reason you originally purchased life insurance (to protect your life), but you've grown into a whole new chapter in life in which there are different, but no less important, reasons to purchase life insurance (to protect your estate and your family). A new chapter in life doesn't erase your need for life insurance, it simply changes your perspective. And in some cases, actually increases the need for life insurance.

So you see, **Single Deposit Insurance is not purchased because of your age, but to properly protect your savings, your spouse, and your heirs.** It's designed specifically to provide for long-term care costs should you have them and will eliminate most, if not all, of the money the Tax Man is waiting to collect. I've never been a fan of divorce in marriage, but I am most definitely a fan of divorcing the Tax Man to eliminate him as my partner for life.

Your money is your money and it should be used to protect and provide for your family. That's now possible by using a properly structured Single Deposit Insurance policy.

*"Live as if you were to die tomorrow.
Learn as if you were to live forever. "*

~ Mahatma Gandhi

7

Looking Forward to Your Future

LOOKING BACK on my life I can honestly say I did a lot of things right. If there's one area I wish I would have done better, it is planning for retirement and what would happen to my family after I died. From the perspective I have now, everything seems so clear.

I know exactly what I would have done to protect my estate and provide for my family. I would find myself a competent, caring financial advisor who specializes in retirement planning. They'd be able to help me set up a properly structured insurance policy that would not only keep out that "uninvited guest," but would also protect me from the unexpected risks by providing for the long-term care needs of my wife should she need it. I'd also make sure to provide her with income for the rest of her life to ensure she is comfortable and insulated from an unpredictable future, and I would leave our children their inheritance tax free.

By using just a little bit of our money (a snowball) I could have created a whole lot more growth (a snowman) and provided a ton of protection for my family. If only . . .

Well, it's too late for me, but not for you. As you are looking forward to your future, let me encourage you to call the advisor who gave you this book and ask them to explain how this might work for you and your family. I'll bet they'll talk with you for free. You have nothing to lose, and a whole lot to gain as you take proactive steps to protecting your future and planning your retirement.

About the Author

Michael Blaker is the founder and president of the nationally-known financial services firm, Senior Consultants. He has been a financial professional since 1985 and has assisted many retirees and pre-retirees in feeling reassured about their retirement income strategies. Family-run Senior Consultants earns satisfaction by instructing financial professionals nationwide in how to use Blaker's highly successful E.S.T.A.T.E. system: Ensuring Seniors Take Advantage of Tax Elimination. You can learn more about Mr. Blaker at www.SeniorConsultants.com.

.